T0398401

CLIMATOLOGY

BY MARTIN HARASYMIW

Gareth Stevens
PUBLISHING

Please visit our website, www.garethstevens.com. For a free color catalog of all our high-quality books, call toll free 1-800-542-2595 or fax 1-877-542-2596.

Cataloging-in-Publication Data
Names: Harasymiw, Martin, 1978-.
Title: Climatology / Martin Harasymiw.
Description: Buffalo, NY : Gareth Stevens Publishing, 2025. | Series: A look at Earth science | Includes glossary and index.
Identifiers: ISBN 9781482467147 (pbk.) | ISBN 9781482467154 (library bound) | ISBN 9781482467161 (ebook)
Subjects: LCSH: Climatology–Juvenile literature. | Climatic changes–Juvenile literature.
Classification: LCC QC863.5 H373 2025 | DDC 551.6–dc23

First Edition

Published in 2025 by
Gareth Stevens Publishing
2544 Clinton Street
Buffalo, NY 14224

Designer: Jennifer Schoembs
Editor: Therese Shea

Photo credits: Cover, p. 1 Al Carrera/Shutterstock.com; series art (ice background) Patricio Estrada/Shutterstock.com; p. 5 peresanz/Shutterstock.com; p. 7 (background) sumroeng chinnapan/Shutterstock.com; pp. 7 (climate map), 23 VectorMine/Shutterstock.com; p. 9 gorillaimages/Shutterstock.com; p. 11 PanyaStudio/Shutterstock.com; p. 13 nullplus/Shutterstock.com; p. 15 (background) ImagesRouges/Shutterstock.com; p. 15 (sunlight diagram) Soleil Nordic/Shutterstock.com; p. 17 Pierre Leclerc/Shutterstock.com; p. 19 (bottom) Fineart1/Shuttersrtock.com; p. 19 (top) NASA/JPL-Caltech/Wikimedia Commons; p. 21 Atmospheric Research/CSIRO/Wikimedia Commons; p. 25 Piyaset/Shutterstock.com; p. 27 shuttermuse/Shutterstock.com; p. 29 Ground Picture/Shutterstock.com.

Printed in the United States of America

Some of the images in this book illustrate individuals who are models. The depictions do not imply actual situations or events.

CPSIA compliance information: Batch #CS25GS: For further information contact Gareth Stevens at 1-800-542-2595.

Find us on

CONTENTS

Weather and Climate 4

Climate Is Key 8

Studying Climate 12

What Causes Climate? 14

Climatology Tools 18

Climate Change and
    Global Warming 22

It's a Big Problem 26

Working for the Future 28

Tasks of a Climatologist 30

Glossary 31

For More Information 32

Index 32

Words in the glossary appear in **bold** type the first time they are used in the text.

WEATHER AND CLIMATE

Weather is what's happening in Earth's **atmosphere** at a certain time. Wind, **temperature**, and cloud cover are all part of the weather. Precipitation is too. That's the name for the different forms of water that fall to the ground, including rain, snow, sleet, and hail.

MAKE THE GRADE How much water is in the air is another part of the weather. This is called humidity.

The weather in a place over time forms **patterns**. Those patterns are called a place's climate. Climate is the **average** weather conditions in a place over a long period of time, often about 30 years. Different places around the world have different climates.

CLIMATE TYPES
KÖPPEN CLIMATE CLASSIFICATION

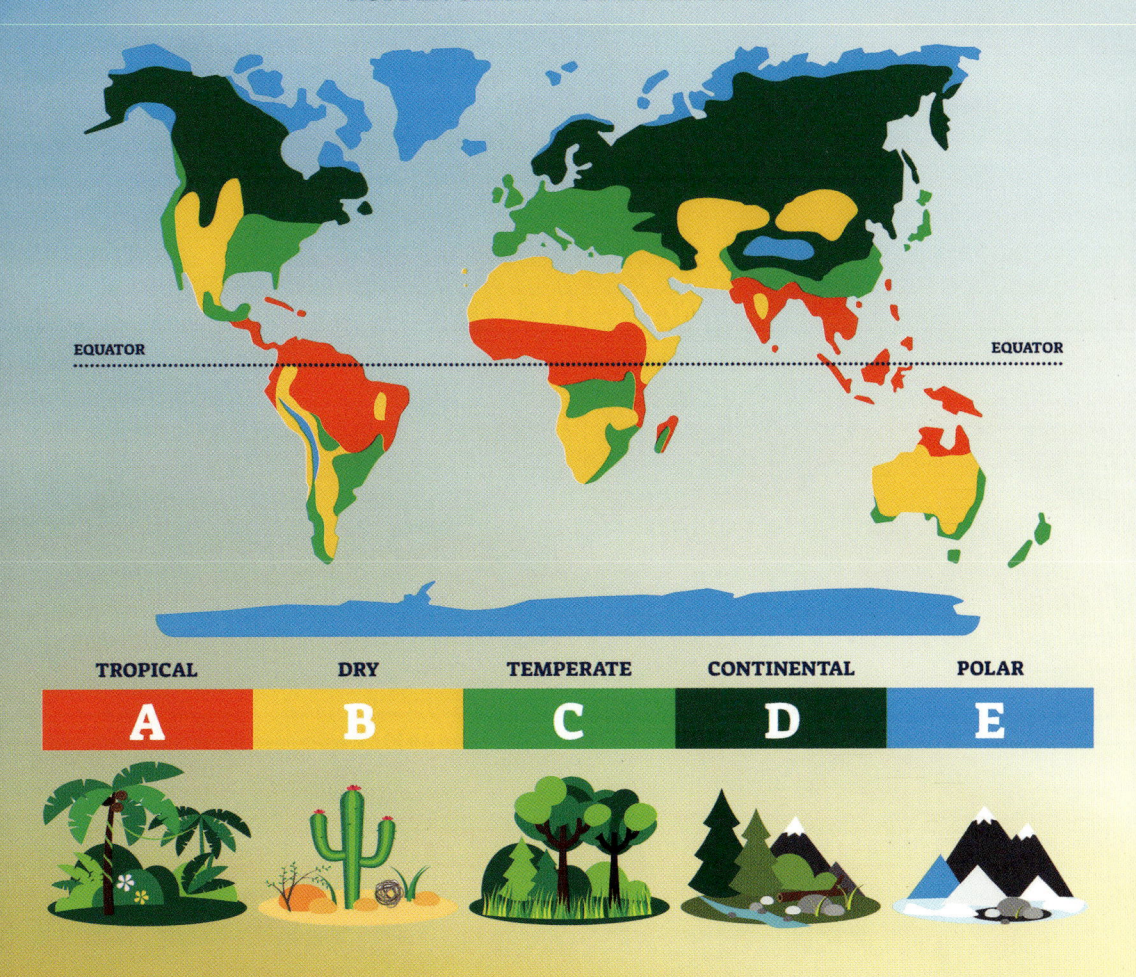

EQUATOR .... EQUATOR

TROPICAL	DRY	TEMPERATE	CONTINENTAL	POLAR
A	**B**	**C**	**D**	**E**

MAKE THE GRADE Climate maps show us the general climate in a place. Continental climates often have a large change in temperature between seasons, such as warm summers and cold winters.

CLIMATE IS KEY

Why is it important to know about climate? Farmers plant the crops you eat according to the climate. Certain crops only grow in certain climates. Farmers use climate **information** to know when to plant and when to pick. They know how much rain to expect too.

MAKE THE GRADE People choose where they live and where they vacation based on climate information. Jobs can depend on climate as well, especially outdoor jobs.

Climate can affect the kinds of clothes we need. People also construct homes and other buildings according to the climate. Energy, or power, companies need to understand climate well. They must be able to provide enough energy to heat or cool people throughout the year.

MAKE THE GRADE Climate affects how energy is produced in different places. Sunny places can produce more solar energy, or power from sunlight. Windy places can use wind to produce energy.

STUDYING CLIMATE

The study of climate is called climatology. Climatologists are scientists who study climate. Some may study climates today. Others study climates of the past. Climatologists can use climate **data** to make **predictions** about future climates and weather events.

MAKE THE GRADE

Some climatologists work in the field, which means studying in nature. Others work in labs and offices.

WHAT CAUSES CLIMATE?

You likely know a bit about the causes of weather. These things affect climate as well. For example, the climate in places near the **equator** is very warm. That's because sunlight hits the equator at a more direct **angle**.

equator

MAKE THE GRADE Places farther from the equator are cooler. They get less powerful sunlight.

Winds affect climate. They carry warm or cold air masses from one place to another. Land features affect climate too. For example, each side of a mountain range can have a different climate. The mountains may stop rain clouds and air masses from reaching places beyond them.

Oceans help create pleasant climates with warm winters and cool summers.

CLIMATOLOGY TOOLS

Climatologists collect information on the ground, in the air, and even from space. They use tools that meteorologists, or weather scientists, use to measure different parts of the weather, including wind speed, temperature, and humidity. They use **satellites** to map weather over larger areas.

The OCO-2 satellite has been measuring the gas called carbon dioxide in the atmosphere since 2014.

weather station

19

Some climatologists study climates from hundreds, thousands, or even millions of years ago. Scientists who study ancient climates are called paleoclimatologists. They search for clues in matter that formed during those time periods, including trees, ice, and rocks.

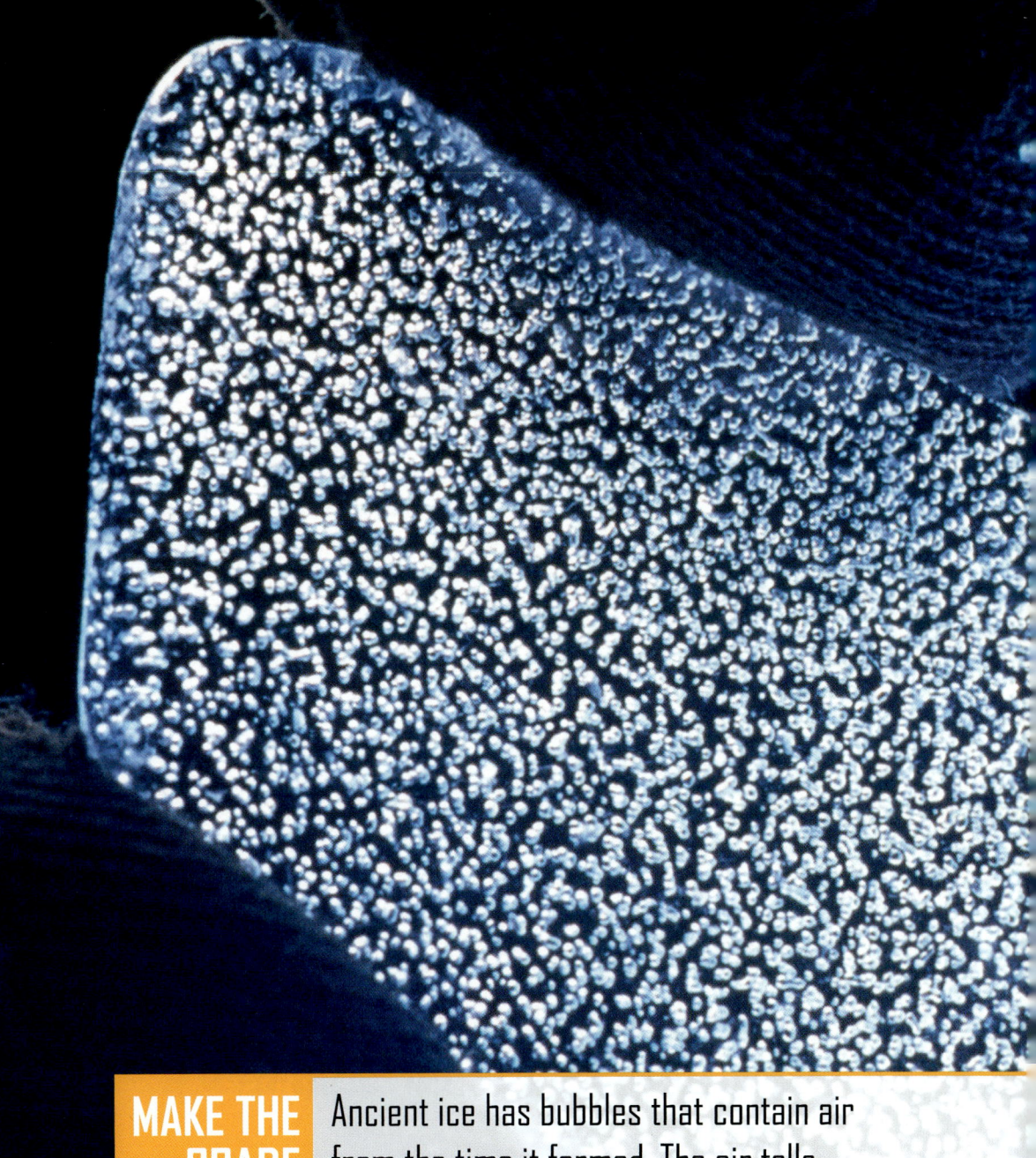

MAKE THE GRADE Ancient ice has bubbles that contain air from the time it formed. The air tells scientists about the atmosphere back then. The oldest **glacier** ice in Antarctica may be 1 million years old!

CLIMATE CHANGE AND GLOBAL WARMING

Climates can change for natural or human-made reasons. Global warming is a part of the climate change happening now. Global warming is the increase, or rise, in average global temperatures around the world. It's linked to the increasing amounts of greenhouse gases in the atmosphere.

Greenhouse Effect

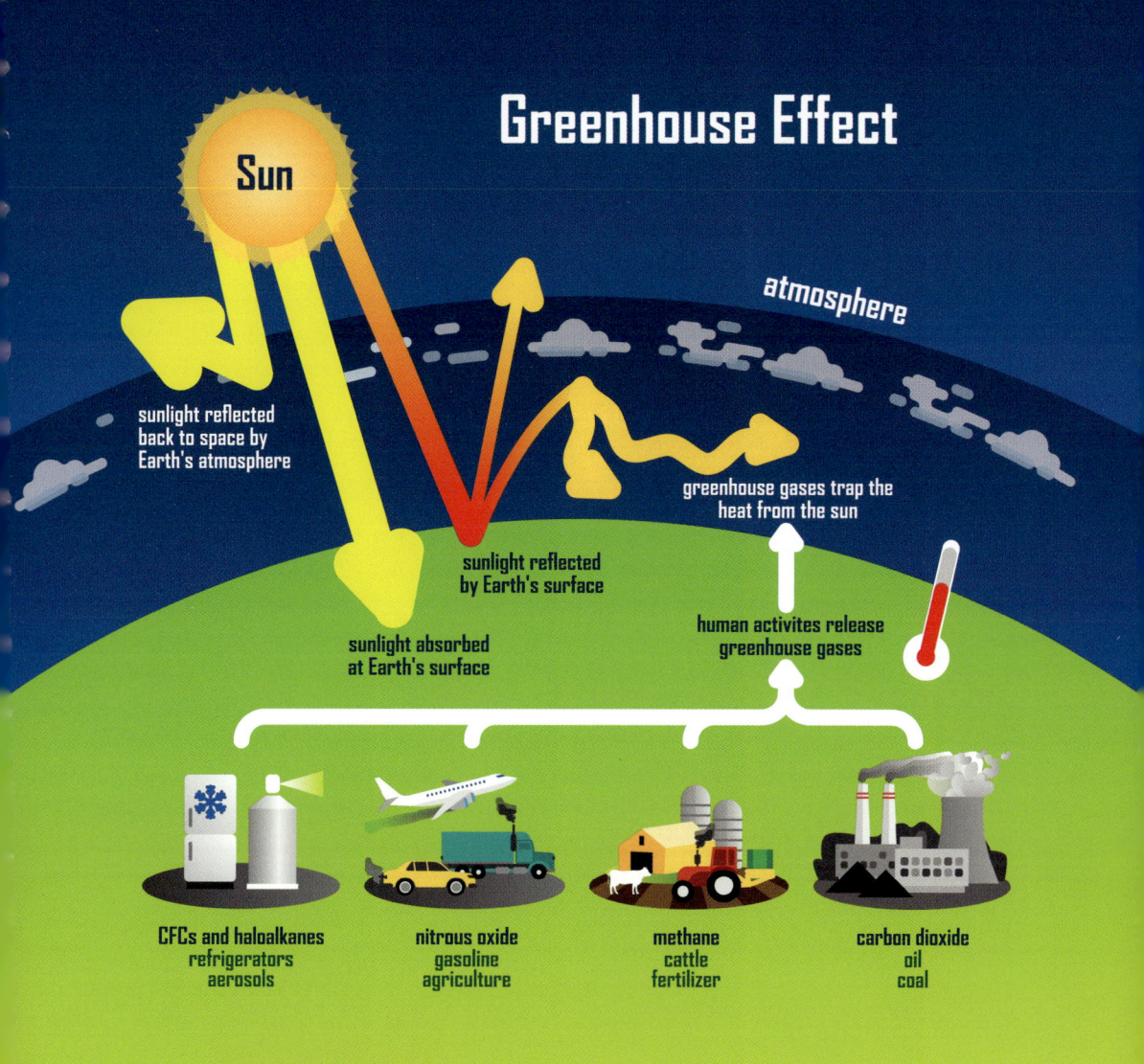

Sun

atmosphere

sunlight reflected back to space by Earth's atmosphere

greenhouse gases trap the heat from the sun

sunlight reflected by Earth's surface

human activites release greenhouse gases

sunlight absorbed at Earth's surface

CFCs and haloalkanes
refrigerators
aerosols

nitrous oxide
gasoline
agriculture

methane
cattle
fertilizer

carbon dioxide
oil
coal

MAKE THE GRADE

A greenhouse gas is any gas in the atmosphere that traps the sun's heat energy. Certain ones, including carbon dioxide and methane, are increasing because of human activities, such as burning **fossil fuels**.

Without greenhouse gases in our atmosphere, we couldn't live on Earth. The problem is the increase in certain gases. Climatologists report the average global temperature increased by about 2°F (1°C) since 1880. That small amount makes a huge difference in global climates.

MAKE THE GRADE

Global warming doesn't mean every place is hotter. One place might be hotter, while another is colder. Global warming is about average global temperature.

IT'S A BIG PROBLEM

Increasing global temperatures are causing major changes around the world. For example, melting glaciers and ice sheets are raising sea levels. Rising sea levels harm people's and animals' coastal homes. Global warming also changes precipitation patterns. It causes more and longer **droughts** and flooding.

MAKE THE GRADE Disappearing sea ice harms polar bears. Polar bears use sea ice to hunt for their food, especially seals.

WORKING FOR THE FUTURE

Without climatology, we wouldn't know climates are changing. We also wouldn't know why. Governments and businesses need climatologists' knowledge as they make choices to battle global warming. This important science can help change our world for the better!

MAKE THE GRADE

The number of needed atmospheric scientists, including climatologists, is expected to increase in the United States by 2030.

TASKS OF A CLIMATOLOGIST

- ✔ *Gather data from weather stations and satellites to study current climates*

- ✔ *Study data, maps, photographs, and charts to predict patterns*

- ✔ *Use computer programs to predict patterns and compare climates*

- ✔ *Predict how climate change may affect certain fields, such as farming or health care*

- ✔ *Do studies to find the reasons behind unusual weather events*

- ✔ *Prepare reports for businesses and governments*

- ✔ *Teach people about climate change*

GLOSSARY

angle: A shape or space formed when two lines or surfaces meet.

atmosphere: The mixture of gases that surround a planet.

average: A number calculated by adding numbers together and then dividing the total by the number of numbers. Also, the usual or typical.

data: Facts and figures.

drought: A long period of very dry weather.

equator: An imaginary line around Earth that is the same distance from the North and South Poles.

fossil fuel: Matter formed over millions of years from plant and animal remains that is burned for power.

glacier: A very large area of slowly moving ice.

information: Knowledge obtained from study or observation.

pattern: The way something happens over and over again.

prediction: A guess about what will happen in the future based on facts or knowledge.

satellite: An object that circles Earth in order to collect and send information or aid in communication.

temperature: How hot or cold something is.

FOR MORE INFORMATION

Books

Earley, Christina. *Climate*. Coral Springs, FL: Seahorse Publishing, 2024.

Woodward, John. *Climate Change.* New York, NY: DK Publishing, 2021.

Website

Weather and Climate
climatekids.nasa.gov/menu/weather-and-climate/
Learn about NASA climate studies going on now.

INDEX

Antarctica, 21

carbon dioxide, 19, 23

clouds, 4, 16

crops, 8

energy, 10

farmers, 8

global temperature, 22, 24, 25, 26

greenhouse gases, 22, 23, 24

humidity, 5, 18

ice, 20, 21, 27

meteorology, 18

mountains, 16

oceans, 17

OCO-2 satellite, 19

paleoclimatology, 20

polar bears, 27

precipitation, 4, 26

rain, 4, 8, 16

rocks, 20

sea level, 26

seasons, 7, 17

space, 18, 19

sun, 10, 14, 15, 23

wind, 4, 10, 16, 18